Don't

Helen Cook
and
Morag Styles

Illustrated by
Errol Lloyd

BUCKINGHAM
MIDDLE
SCHOOL

CAMBRIDGE
UNIVERSITY PRESS

PUBLISHED BY THE PRESS SYNDICATE OF THE UNIVERSITY OF CAMBRIDGE
The Pitt Building, Trumpington Street, Cambridge CB2 1RP, United Kingdom

CAMBRIDGE UNIVERSITY PRESS
The Edinburgh Building, Cambridge CB2 2RU, United Kingdom
40 West 20th Street, New York, NY 10011-4211, USA
10 Stamford Road, Oakleigh, Melbourne 3166, Australia

First published 1991
Reprinted 1998

Printed in the United Kingdom at the University Press, Cambridge

Typeset in Photina

A catalogue record for this book is available from the British Library

ISBN 0 521 39952 1   paperback

Acknowledgements

'Kids' from *Startling Verse for All the Family* by Spike Milligan, copyright © Spike Milligan Productions; 'Don't' from *Don't Put Mustard in the Custard* by Michael Rosen, André Deutsch 1986; 'I Woke Up This Morning' from *Dogs and Dragons, Trees and Dreams* by Karla Kuskin. Originally published in *The Rose on My Cake* by Karla Kuskin. Copyright © 1964 by Karla Kuskin; 'Suzanna Socked Me Sunday' from *The New Kid on the Block* by Jack Prelutsky, William Heinemann Ltd 1986 and William Morrow & Co Inc; 'Bossy Parrot' © Emma Reid; 'Parents Never Understand' from *Spin a Soft Black Song* by Nikki Giovanni. Copyright © 1971, 1985 by Nikki Giovanni, reprinted by permission of Farrar, Straus & Giroux, Inc.; 'Monday's Child' from *There's an Awful Lot of Weirdos in Our Neighbourhood*, copyright © 1987 Colin McNaughton, first published in the UK by Walker Books Ltd; 'A-So it Go' by kind permission of John Agard c/o Caroline Sheldon Literary Agency, from *Laughter is an Egg* published by Viking Kestrel 1989; 'Dave Dirt Came to Dinner' by Kit Wright, from *Hot Dog and Other Poems* by Kit Wright (Kestrel, 1981), copyright © Kit Wright, 1981; Errol Lloyd for 'Blame the Parents'; 'Teacher Said . . .' reprinted by permission of Faber & Faber Ltd, from *Magic Mirror* by Judith Nicholls; 'Twiddling Your Thumbs' reprinted by permission of Faber & Faber Ltd from *Twiddling Your Thumbs* by Wendy Cope; 'Never' by Rebecca Halliday reprinted by permission of The Blackstaff Press; 'Don't Call Alligator Longmouth Till You Cross the River' from *Say it Again, Granny* by John Agard. The Bodley Head 1986; 'Good Morning, Mr Croco-doco-dile' from *Early in the Morning* by Charles Causley, Viking Kestrel 1986; 'Come Out With Me' from *Now We Are Six* by A A Milne. Copyright © 1927 by E.P. Dutton, renewed 1955 by A A Milne. Reprinted by permission of the publisher, Dutton Children's Books, a division of Penguin Books USA Inc., and Methuen Children's Books; 'Father and I in the Woods' from *One at a Time* by David McCord. Copyright 1952 by David McCord. By permission of Harrap & Co and Little, Brown and Co; an extract from 'Clearances' reprinted by permission of Faber & Faber Ltd from *The Haw Lantern* by Seamus Heaney; 'Rules' by Brian Patten, from *Gargling with Jelly* by Brian Patten (Kestrel, 1985), copyright © Brian Patten, 1985.

Every effort has been made to reach copyright holders; the publishers would be glad to hear from anyone whose rights they have unknowingly infringed.

Contents

Kids

'Sit up straight,'
Said mum to Mabel.
'Keep your elbows
Off the table.
Do not eat peas
Off a fork.
Your mouth is full –
Don't try and talk.
Keep your mouth shut
When you eat.
Keep still or you'll
Fall off your seat.
If you want more,
You will say "please".
Don't fiddle with
That piece of cheese!'
If then we kids
Cause such a fuss,
Why do you go on
Having us?

Spike Milligan

Don't

Don't do,
Don't do,
Don't do that.
Don't pull faces,
Don't tease the cat.

Don't pick your ears,
Don't be rude at school.
Who do they think I am?

Some kind of fool?

One day
they'll say
Don't put toffee in my coffee
don't pour gravy on the baby
don't put beer in his ear
don't stick your toes up his nose.

Don't put confetti on the spaghetti
and don't squash peas on your knees.

Don't put ants in your pants
don't put mustard in the custard

don't chuck jelly at the telly

and don't throw fruit at the computer
don't throw fruit at the computer.

Don't what?
Don't throw fruit at the computer.
Don't what?
Don't throw fruit at the computer.
Who do they think I am?
Some kind of fool?

Michael Rosen

I Woke Up This Morning

I woke up this morning
At quarter past seven.
I kicked up the covers
And stuck out my toe.
And ever since then
(That's a quarter past seven)
They haven't said anything
Other than 'no'.

They haven't said anything
Other than 'Please, dear,
Don't do what you're doing,'
Or 'Lower your voice.'
And however I've chosen,
I've done the wrong thing
And I've made the wrong choice.

I didn't wash well
And I didn't say thank you.
I didn't shake hands
And I didn't say please.
I didn't say sorry
When, passing the candy,
I banged the box into
Miss Witelson's knees.
I didn't say sorry.
I didn't stand straighter.
I didn't speak louder
When asked what I'd said.

Well, I said
That tomorrow
At quarter past seven,
They can
Come in and get me
I'M STAYING IN BED.

Karla Kuskin

Suzanna Socked Me Sunday

Suzanna socked me Sunday,
she socked me Monday, too,
she also socked me Tuesday,
I was turning black and blue.

She socked me double Wednesday,
and Thursday even more,
but when she socked me Friday,
she began to get me sore.

'Enough's enough,' I yelled at her,
'I hate it when you hit me!'
'Well, then I won't!' Suzanna said –
that Saturday, she bit me.

Jack Prelutsky

Bossy Parrot (My Sister)

Mum said, PIANO! Emma,
   Bossy Parrot said, Mum said piano!

Mum said, BATH! Emma,
   Bossy Parrot said, Mum said bath!

Mum said, SUPPER! Emma,
   Bossy Parrot said, Mum said supper!

That does it, I said.
Homework!! Move your blazer!
Move your bag!
My sister is a Bossy Parrot!!!

Emma Reid (aged 9)

Parents Never Understand

well i can't 'cause
yesterday when mommy had
this important visitor she said
run along joey and let mommy talk
and i ran along upstairs to see
bobby and eddie and we were playing
and forgot and i had to come down
stairs and get dry clothes and mommy said how
could an eight year old boy wet his pants
and i looked at the visitor and smiled a really nice
smile and said i guess in america anything
can happen
so mommy said i have to
stay in today   *Nikki Giovanni*

Monday's Child is Red and Spotty

Monday's child is red and spotty,
Tuesday's child won't use the potty.
Wednesday's child won't go to bed,
Thursday's child will not be fed.
Friday's child breaks all his toys,
Saturday's child makes an awful noise.
And the child that's born on the seventh day
Is a pain in the neck like the rest, OK!

Colin McNaughton

A-So It Go

So mouthy-mouthy
so mouthy-mouthy
you got so much
MOUTHABILITY!
A-so it go
A-so it go
when yuh mouth can't stop flow

So wanty-wanty
so wanty-wanty
you got so much
WANTABILITY!
A-so it go
A-so it go
when you wanty dis and wanty dat

So laughy-laughy
so laughy-laughy
you got so much
LAUGHABILITY!
Take care one day you laughy-laughy
till you burst
yuh belly-belly

John Agard

A Rhyme for a Nosey Parker

Ask no questions
And you'll be told no lies;
Shut your mouth
And you'll catch no flies.

Anon

Policeman, Policeman

Policeman, policeman
   don't catch me!
Catch that boy
   behind that tree.
He stole apples,
   I stole none;
Put him in the jailhouse,
   just for fun.

Anon

Dave Dirt Came to Dinner

Dave Dirt came to dinner
   And he stuck his chewing gum
Underneath the table
   And it didn't please my Mum

And it didn't please my Granny
   Who was quite a sight to see
When she got up from the table
   With the gum stuck to her knee

Where she put her cup and saucer
   When she sat and drank her tea
And the saucer and the chewing gum
   Got stuck as stuck can be

And she staggered round the kitchen
   With a saucer on her skirt –
No, it didn't please my Granny
   But it
     PLEASED
      DAVE
       DIRT

Kit Wright

17

Blame the Parents

I blame the parents
said Miss,
I really do.
They just don't know how to say no.
They don't know how to say no
to TV
They don't know how to say no
to videos
They don't know how to say no
to bike riding
They don't know how to say no
to playing outside
They don't know how to say no
to ice-cream
They don't know how to say no
to karate.
I wouldn't
send my child to karate.
Would you?

Errol Lloyd

Teacher Said . . .

You can use
   mumbled and muttered,
   groaned, grumbled and uttered,
   professed, droned or stuttered
          . . . but *don't* use SAID!

You can use
   rant or recite,
   yell, yodel or snort,
   bellow, murmur or moan,
   you can grunt or just groan
          . . . but *don't* use SAID!

You can
   hum, howl and hail,
   scream, screech, shriek or bawl,
   squeak, snivel or squeal
   with a blood-curdling wail
          . . . but *don't* use SAID!

          . . . SAID my teacher.

          Judith Nicholls

19

Twiddling Your Thumbs

When you've finished all your writing
And you've got stuck with your sums
And you need to see your teacher
But your turn never comes,
You may have time to practise this –
Twiddling your thumbs.

Round and round and round they go,
Forwards, backwards, fast or slow,
Then, if you should get the chance,
Make them do a little dance.

When you've eaten up your dinner,
Including all the crumbs,
And you're waiting for permission
To go out with your chums,
Here's a way to pass the time –
Twiddling your thumbs.

Round and round and round they go,
Forwards, backwards, fast or slow,
Then, if you should get the chance,
Make them do a little dance.

If you have to go out visiting
With aunts and dads and mums
And its boring being with grown-ups
All sitting on their bums,
Don't scream and bite the carpet –
Try twiddling your thumbs.

Round and round and round they go,
Forwards, backwards, fast or slow,
Then, if you should get the chance,
Make them do a little dance.

Wendy Cope

Never

Mummy says never run on the road.
Daddy says never cheat.
My brother says never play with his toys.
Nanny says never kiss the boys.
Grandad says never a secret tell.
I'm sick, sore and tired of being told,
     Never!

Rebecca Halliday (aged 8)

Burp

Pardon me
for being so rude.
It was not me
It was my food.
It just came up
to say hallo.
Now it's gone
back down below.

Anon

Mother Made a Seedy Cake

Mother made a seedy cake,
Gave us all the belly ache;
Father bought a pint of beer,
Gave us all the diarrhoea.

Playground rhyme

Don't Call Alligator Long-Mouth
Till You Cross River

Call alligator long-mouth
call alligator saw-mouth
call alligator pushy-mouth
call alligator scissors-mouth
call alligator raggedy-mouth
call alligator bumpy-bum
call alligator all dem rude word
but better wait
                till you cross river.

                        John Agard

Good Morning, Mr Croco-doco-dile

Good morning, Mr Croco-doco-dile,
And how are you today?
I like to see you croco-smoco-smile
In your croco-woco-way.

From the tip of your beautiful croco-toco-tail
To your croco-hoco-head
You seem to me so croco-stoco-still
As if you're croco-doco-dead.

Perhaps if I touch your croco-cloco-claw
Or your croco-snoco-snout,
Or get up close to your croco-joco-jaw
I shall very soon find out.

But suddenly I croco-soco-see
In your croco-oco-eye
A curious kind of croco-gloco-gleam,
So I just don't think I'll try.

Forgive me, Mr Croco-doco-dile
But it's time I was away.
Let's talk a little croco-woco-while
Another croco-doco-day.

Charles Causley

Come Out with Me

There's sun on the river and sun on the hill . . .
You can hear the sea if you stand quite still!
There's eight new puppies at Roundabout Farm –
And I saw an old sailor with only one arm!

But every one says, 'Run along!'
(Run along, run along!)
All of them say 'Run along! I'm busy as can be.'
Every one says, 'Run along,
There's a little darling!'
If I'm a little darling, why don't they run with me?

There's wind on the river and wind on the hill . . .
There's a dark dead water-wheel under the mill!
I saw a fly which had just been drowned –
And I know where a rabbit goes into the ground!

But every one says, 'Run along!'
(Run along, run along!)
All of them say 'Yes, dear,' and never notice me.
Every one says, 'Run along,
There's a little darling!'
If I'm a little darling, why won't they come and see?

A A Milne

Father and I in the Woods

'Son,'
My father used to say,
'Don't run.'

'Walk,'
My father used to say,
'Don't talk.'

'Words,'
My father used to say,
'Scare birds.'

So be:
It's sky and brook and bird
And tree.

David McCord

Polished linoleum shone there. Brass taps shone.
The china cups were very white and big –
An unchipped set with sugar bowl and jug.
The kettle whistled. Sandwich and teascone
Were present and correct. In case it run,
The butter must be kept out of the sun.
And don't be dropping crumbs. Don't tilt your chair.
Don't reach. Don't point. Don't make noise when you stir.

Seamus Heaney

Rules

Governments rule most countries,
Bankers rule most banks,
Captains rule their football teams
And piranhas rule fish tanks.

There are rules for gnobling gnomes
And rules for frying frogs,
There are rules for biting bullies
And for vexing vicious dogs.

There are rules for driving motor cars
And crashing into chums,
There are rules for taking off your pants
And showing spotty bums.

There are rules for nasty children
Who tie bangers to old cats,
There are rules for running riot
And rules for burning bats.

There are rules in the classroom.
There are rules in the street.
Some rules are wild and woolly
And some are tame and neat.

And some are pretty sensible
And some are pretty daft;
Some I take quite seriously,
At others I have laughed,

But there is one special rule
You should not be without:
If you do not like the rules
OPEN YOUR MOUTH AND SHOUT!
OPEN YOUR MOUTH AND SHOUT!

Brian Patten

Speak Roughly to Your Little Boy

Speak roughly to your little boy
   And beat him when he sneezes:
He only does it to annoy,
   Because he knows it teases.

CHORUS
Wow! wow! wow!

I speak severely to my boy,
   I beat him when he sneezes;
For he can thoroughly enjoy
   The pepper when he pleases!

CHORUS
Wow! wow! wow!

Lewis Carroll